D1442051

MARTIAL ARTS

KENDO

by Tim O'Shei

Reading Consultant:
Barbara J. Fox
Reading Specialist
North Carolina State University

Content Consultant:
David T. Christman, 4th Degree Black Belt
Member, All United States Kendo Federation
Founder, Battle Creek Kendo Kai
Battle Creek, Michigan

Capstone
press

Mankato, Minnesota

Blazers is published by Capstone Press,
151 Good Counsel Drive, P.O. Box 669, Mankato, Minnesota 56002.
www.capstonepress.com

Library of Congress Cataloging-in-Publication Data
O'Shei, Tim.
        Kendo / by Tim O'Shei.
        p. cm. — (Blazers. Martial arts)
        Summary: "Discusses the history, techniques, ranks, and competitions of
kendo" — Provided by publisher.
        Includes bibliographical references and index.
        ISBN-13: 978-1-4296-1964-6 (hardcover)
        ISBN-10: 1-4296-1964-3 (hardcover)
        1. Kendo — Juvenile literature. I. Title.
GV1142.O84 2009
796.86 — dc22   2007052198

Essential content terms are **bold** and are defined on the spread where they first appear.

Editorial Credits
Abby Czeskleba, editor; Ted Williams, designer; Jo Miller, photo researcher;
      Sarah L. Schuette, photo shoot direction; Marcy Morin, scheduler

Photo Credits
All photography in this book by Capstone Press/Karon Dubke except:
Alamy/Frances M. Roberts, 24–25
Getty Images Inc./Hulton Archive/Kusakabe Kimbei, 4–5

The Capstone Press Photo Studio thanks the Rochester YMCA and the members of
the Hokkyokusei Kendo Club of Rochester, Minnesota, for their assistance with photo
shoots for this book.

The author thanks Emily Warne for her assistance with this book.

1 2 3 4 5 6 13 12 11 10 09 08

TABLE OF CONTENTS

CHAPTER 1
THE BEGINNING OF KENDO

Hundreds of years ago, sword masters fought battles in Japan. These sword masters were Japanese soldiers called samurai.

In 1877, government fighters defeated the samurai in the Satsuma Rebellion. Today, people practice kendo. They use some of the same sword skills as the samurai. Kendo is most popular in Japan.

MARTIAL ARTS FACT

Kendo is Japanese sword fighting. It means "the way of the sword."

CHAPTER 2

PRACTICING KENDO

Fighters wear special pants and a jacket. They may also wear armor during practice. Fighters do not wear armor when practicing with **bokken**.

MARTIAL ARTS FACT

A fighter's protective armor is called *bogu*. Custom-made bogu can cost up to $10,000!

bokken — a solid wood sword used to practice basic moves

A fighter moves with the knees bent and the left foot back. The right foot faces the other fighter. This foot position helps a fighter move quickly.

Kendo fighters are called *kendoka*.

Kendo students use bokken to practice new moves slowly and carefully. They learn moves from their **sensei**. Students must always respect their sensei.

MARTIAL ARTS FACT

Some of the lightsaber battles in the *Star Wars* movies are based on kendo moves.

sensei — the Japanese word for teacher

13

Fighters practice a set of movements called **kata**. First, fighters bow to show respect. Then, they raise their bokken and move toward each other.

MARTIAL ARTS FACT

There are a total of 10 kata. Fighters learn more of the kata as their skills improve.

kata — a set of movements used in kendo

15

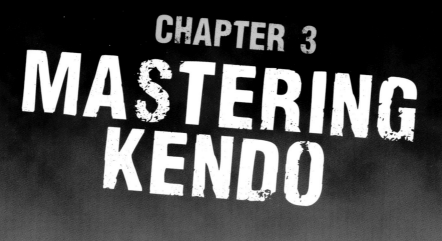

CHAPTER 3
MASTERING KENDO

Students with basic skills have the rank of *kyu*. There are six levels of kyu. Fighters earn new ranks by showing their skills in tests.

北極星
賛美悟
SANTIAGO

北極星
飯島
R.IIJIMA

17

After kyu comes the rank of *dan*. Dan is equal to a black belt in karate. There are eight levels of dan. It can take more than 30 years to reach the highest level.

KENDO DIAGRAM

SHINAI

PADDED GLOVES

FACE MASK

JACKET

CHEST PROTECTOR

21

CHAPTER 4
KENDO COMPETITIONS

It's competition time! The match begins with two fighters bowing. Fighters use **shinai** to earn points in a match. When fighters attack, they yell out a body part as they strike it.

shinai — a sword made of a light, woody plant called bamboo

A kendo match usually lasts five minutes. The first fighter to score two points wins the match. Fighters earn points by striking the head, neck, wrist, or chest.

MARTIAL ARTS FACT

Fighters cannot earn points if they are touching their opponents before they strike.

Kendo fighters practice for the World Kendo Championship (WKC). The WKC takes place every three years. Fighters from 49 countries attended the 2006 WKC. The samurai may be gone, but their sword skills live on through kendo.

MARTIAL ARTS FACT

The U.S. men's team earned second place in the 2006 World Kendo Championship. South Korea took first place.

Kendo fighters practice their skills for the World Kendo Championship.

北極星
基
納
KEENER

SHINAI STRIKE!

GLOSSARY

armor (AR-muhr) — equipment used to protect a kendo fighter

bokken (BOH-ken) — a solid wood sword used to practice basic moves; fighters do not hit each other with bokken.

kata (KAH-tah) — a set of movements used in kendo; a kata is full of sword strikes and blocks.

opponent (uh-POH-nuhnt) — a person who competes against another person in a fight or contest

samurai (SAH-muh-rye) — Japanese warriors who fought in battles between the years 500 and 1877

Satsuma Rebellion (sat-SOO-muh ri-BEL-yuhn) — the final battle of the samurai; the 60,000 government fighters defeated the 20,000 samurai in 1877.

sensei (SEN-say) — the Japanese word for teacher

shinai (shee-NAH-ee) — a sword made of a light, woody plant called bamboo; kendo fighters use shinai to strike each other during a competition.

READ MORE

Carter, Kevin. *Martial Arts for Fun!* Activities for Fun. Minneapolis: Compass Point Books, 2004.

Dean, Arlan. *Samurai: Warlords of Japan.* Way of the Warrior. New York: Children's Press, 2005.

Macdonald, Fiona. *How to Be a Samurai Warrior.* How to Be Series. Washington, D.C.: National Geographic, 2005.

INTERNET SITES

FactHound offers a safe, fun way to find Internet sites related to this book. All of the sites on FactHound have been researched by our staff.

Here's how:
1. Visit *www.facthound.com*
2. Choose your grade level.
3. Type in this book ID **1429619643** for age-appropriate sites. You may also browse subjects by clicking on letters, or by clicking on pictures and words.
4. Click on the **Fetch It** button.

FactHound will fetch the best sites for you!

INDEX